Communicating Spiritual Values Through Christian Music

AL MENCONI

LIFEJOURNEY
BOOKS

LifeJourney Books is an imprint of David C. Cook
Publishing Co.
David C. Cook Publishing Co., Elgin, Illinois 60120
David C. Cook Publishing Co., Weston, Ontario
Nova Distribution, Ltd., Torquay, England

Communicating Spiritual Values Through Christian Music
©1991 by Al Menconi
(This booklet consists of selected portions of *Today's
Music: Window to Your Child's Soul* ©1990 by Al
Menconi with Dave Hart)

Edited by Brian Reck
Cover design by Bob Fuller
First printing, 1991
Printed in the United States of America
95 94 93 92 91 5 4 3 2 1

Library of Congress Cataloging in Publication Data
Menconi, Al
Communicating Spiritual Values Through Christian Music/
Al Menconi
    p. cm. — (Helping Families Grow series)
ISBN: 1-55513-658-3
Christian education—Home training. 2. Contemporary
Christian music—History and criticism. 3. Evangelicalism.
4. Family—Religious life.   I. Title.   II. Series: Helping
Families Grow.
BV1590.M46   1991
246'.7—dc20   91-26598
                                CIP

"These commandments . . . are to be upon your hearts. Impress them on your children"
(Deuteronomy 6:6-7).

At a major evangelical church in northern California, I was challenging the congregation to incorporate Christian music into their everyday lives at home. To communicate a point to the parents, I said to the young people in the congregation, "Kids, fill in the blank. Christian music is _____." With one voice, they answered, "Boring!"

The parents couldn't believe it. You could see it on their faces: "Not only do our children listen to the enemy's music, but they think our music is boring. With this attitude, how are we ever going to get them to listen to Christian music?"

These families were in one of the largest and strongest Christian churches in that area, and I get the same response at most other churches where I speak. Adults everywhere tend to assume that new Christians and young people automatically enjoy traditional church music. It has never occurred to many church parents that it takes time and effort to teach young people to value and enjoy Christian music.

Jesus once described a man who cast a demon out of his house. Then he cleaned his house and put it in order, but left it unattended. The empty, unguarded house was filled with seven demons when he returned, and his condition was worse than ever (Luke 11:24-26). It is not enough to simply remove the demons of rock music. We must fill the void with something positive and equally dynamic.

I have seen many people, young and old, decide to throw out their secular music, but then reverse their decisions later on. And when they do go back to secular music, they are usually even more devoted to it. Their intentions were good, but they didn't find a positive replacement for the music they gave up.

As a child begins to let go of secular music and media, parents must make a definite effort to fill the void left. We would do well to review Deuteronomy 6:7, which instructs us to use every opportunity to teach children the commandments of God. We are to impress them on our children. We are to discuss them when we are at home, as we walk along the road, when we lie down, and when we get up.

This can be a convicting picture in regard to our lives today. Many church families do not think much about God, and they may actually be focusing on the things of Satan through their choice of entertainment. When they sit at home, they absorb empty philosophies through television or secular music. When they go along the road, they cruise to the emptiness blasting from their car stereos. When they lie down and get up, their clock radios focus on the values of this present age instead of the age to come.

How do we get our families to change their focus? How do we get our kids to focus their minds about the things of God if they believe Christian music is boring? We must teach the value of Christian music. It is our responsibility as parents to convince our children that Christian music can be exciting and dynamic, and that the Gospel it presents can cut like a two-edged sword.

SHARING YOUR TESTIMONY SONG

There is hope. One way to cultivate a taste for Christian music is through a testimony song. This is a song that expresses your love for God and describes your walk with the Lord. It doesn't necessarily express who God is or describe the great things that He does. Rather, it should be a song that expresses how you personally feel about your relationship with God. A testimony song lets someone else understand *why* you love Jesus. Every Christian should have a testimony song.

Select a song that accurately describes the feelings you have in your soul for Jesus, not one you think your children will like. You aren't likely to find a true testimony song that will also entertain your children. A mature adult and a young child rarely have the same taste in music.

My first testimony song was "Heaven Came Down and Glory Filled My Soul." The first time I heard it, I got all excited. I thought, *That's it! That's exactly what happened to me in 1971 when I committed my life to Jesus Christ. It was like heaven came down and glory filled my soul!*

Several years later I heard a B. J. Thomas song called "He Gave Me Love When No One Gave Me a Prayer." It made me recall my spiritual struggle during the time after my mother was hospitalized. Because of my ungodly college life-style, all my Christian friends had given up on me and quit praying for me. And my mother was too sick to pray for me as she had for so long. But God in His mercy and grace chose to love me and save me anyway. God gave me love when (literally) *no one* gave me a prayer.

That song illustrated my past, but I also like to look to my future. My children are my future. When I heard the song "Somewhere in the World" on the *Giants in the Land* album by Wayne Watson, it became my most inspiring testimony song. The challenge of the song is to pray for the person your child will marry someday. This is something my wife and I have done ever since our daughters were toddlers.

Why pray for their future husbands even while our daughters are little girls? Because somewhere in the world those future husbands—whoever they are—are little boys. With the pressures to conform to this world, those little boys need a lot of prayer. If it's tough to have a successful marriage now, imagine how difficult it will be by the time they are adults. I want my daughters to live for Jesus as adults and to have successful marriages, and Wayne Watson's song reminds me to keep praying. Even though I don't even know who I'm praying for, God does.

Don't pick your song too quickly. Many parents want to choose a favorite hymn because it's familiar and easy. But I would like to challenge you to listen to a lot of different Christian songs and artists. Listen until you find one that precisely expresses your love for Jesus.

When you find an appropriate song, ask your kids for five minutes of their time. Explain that you would like to have them listen to a song that means a lot to you. Take one of your five minutes to give a little background and why you chose this song. Then have them read the lyrics with you while the song is played. Make sure they focus on the message of the song instead of its sound. Do your best to make this a pleasant experience, and don't force participation if you haven't been communicating well up to this point.

The goal is to allow your family to share what you feel in your soul and to see your love for Jesus. Follow the song with a question or two. Don't ask, "Did you like that?" or "Wasn't that cool?" Ask instead, "Now do you understand why I love Jesus?" or "Do you understand a little more about why I am a Christian? This is very important to me."

This exercise can accomplish a number of things. First, it shows your children at least one Christian song that isn't boring. The music may not have been their favorite style, but they begin to see Christian music as something personal, deep, and interesting. This may be a new experience for them.

Second, you model vulnerability by exposing your innermost spiritual feelings to your child. If you're ever going to introduce your children to Jesus, they have to understand why you love Him. Be willing to discuss any issues that arise from listening to your testimony song. Be prepared to extend the five minutes to as long as it takes to answer questions and finish the discussion.

Third, children often begin to think of songs that speak personally to them. Whenever I give this challenge during a seminar, many people begin to think through their library of songs for one that explains their love for Jesus. Your children are likely to have the same response.

Finally, your child will subconsciously learn to evaluate his own music for ministry value. Up to this time, he may have thought of music simply as a means of entertainment. Now he will begin to understand that music can be more. It can also be ministry.

By the way, these principles can easily be applied to a group. I hear from pastors, Christian schoolteachers, youth workers, Sunday school teachers, and others who have utilized the principles and techniques of the testimony song with great success.

CHRISTIAN MUSIC AS A TEACHING TOOL

Christian music can be a springboard to launch all sorts of discussions about personal and spiritual values with young people. It can help us talk to our children, listen to them, understand them better, and help them work through the values, morals, and spiritual issues in their lives. Parents and other caring adults want to communicate with children, but find it difficult to relate to a younger generation. That's why I encourage adults to use Christian music as a communication tool.

Studies show that the average father offers his children *less than five minutes* of effective communication each day. Mothers average only slightly more. The problem may not be that the parents don't *want* to communicate with their children. Maybe they don't know how, because sometimes it can be like pulling teeth.

I have to be honest. I don't have much in common with my daughters. They're girls and I'm not. They're preteens and I'm over 40. I do my very best to develop common interests, but sometimes they just don't want to talk. Sometimes they don't believe I'm going to listen anyway. Sometimes I don't ask the right questions. Sometimes I talk about things that interest me rather than things that interest them. But I keep trying.

My desire is to be better than the average father who talks to his child less than five minutes a day. Sometimes when I get lax, my wife challenges me, "Al, why don't you put in your five minutes today?" So I pick up my daughters at school, ready and eager to communicate. Here's one of our typical "deep" discussions.

"Hi, Allison. Did you have fun today?"
"Yes."
"What did you do?"
"Played."

"Oh. Well, what did you do besides play?"

"Schoolwork."

"Well, tell me, what's the first thing you did?"

"Studied the Bible."

"Which part?"

"About Daniel."

"What did you learn about Daniel?"

"Lions' den."

"How about math?"

"We did arithmetic."

"What did you learn in arithmetic?"

"Fractions."

"What did you learn about fractions?"

"We learned what a numerator and a denominator was."

"What else are you studying?"

"Missions in California history."

"What about the missions?"

"San Diego was the first."

This exchange was an actual conversation. I consider myself to be above average in communication skills. In fact, my ministry depends on my ability to communicate. But I've come to realize that the only thing I have in common with my children is that we all love their mother.

Thankfully, I have found that I don't

have to depend on "out of the blue" conversations to communicate with my daughters. I have discovered how to use Christian music to initiate some wonderful times of discussion. Sharing Christian music with my daughters has helped me understand how they think, how they feel, and who they are. I have seen sides of them I never saw before. I have been able to discuss things with them that I would have no idea how to bring up otherwise. I have been able to talk about spiritual truth in very natural ways.

Actually, I discovered this quite by accident. When my older daughter was six, we were in the car listening to a Leslie Phillips song from her album, *Beyond Saturday Night*. The song was called "Gina." As we drove down the freeway, Leslie sang about her friend Gina, who had been killed in an automobile accident before Leslie had a chance to tell her about Jesus.

I didn't realize that Ann was listening, but suddenly she said, "Daddy, does that mean that Gina went to hell?"

Ann's question hit me like a ton of bricks. I was stunned. I had to say, "Yes, if she didn't know Jesus, the Bible tells us she would go to hell."

"Why didn't Leslie tell Gina about Jesus, if she knew Gina was going to hell if she died?" Ann asked.

"Well," I said, "I guess Leslie figured that she had more time, but actually she didn't." At that point, I was able to talk to my daughter about heaven and hell, along with other important things from the Word of God.

Our conversation had a dramatic effect on how my daughter related to others. From that point on she wouldn't play long with new friends before asking them, "Do you know Jesus? Do you go to church? Are you a Christian?" She was afraid that her friends might die before she told them about Jesus.

Our conversation also a had a dramatic impact on me. I realized that I could discuss life-changing issues with my daughters through music. Ann was willing to listen because she brought up the topic. Who knows if she listens when I try to lecture at her? But with music as the catalyst, I had a wonderful opportunity to talk to her about significant issues. Since then, Christian music has led to many other opportunities to communicate God's truth to both my daughters.

But playing Christian music doesn't

automatically guarantee good communication. Sometimes it takes a little work. A few years later, I was on a speaking tour, traveling with my family in a motor home. While we were driving through the Midwestern plains, we happened to be listening to a Russ Taff song from his *Medals* album called, "Not Gonna Bow." I was enjoying it, pleased to be a neat Christian father encouraging my neat little Christian daughters to listen to this neat Christian music, which I knew had a tremendous spiritual message.

"Ann," I said, "do you like that song?"

"Yes," she replied.

"Do you know what it means?"

She looked at me and said, "No."

That's when it hit me. I was listening to a song's spiritual content and being ministered to. But I was a mature adult. My daughter, who was spiritually less mature, was listening only because it had a sound that she enjoyed. She didn't understand the message.

What should a father do in a case like that? Should he criticize his daughter for listening to music just because she likes the sound? Or does he take that opportunity to explain the significance of the message to her? I chose the latter. I began explaining the spiritual significance of "Not Gonna Bow" to my daughter. I reviewed the story of Shadrach, Meshach, and Abednego mentioned in the song.

The song tells how a young boy named Bobby was asked to compromise his faith by giving in to the things of the world. All his friends said, "Come on, Bobby, won't you be like us? Come on, Bobby, what's the fuss?"

But Bobby said, "No, I'm not gonna to bow."

I explained to Ann how the experience of Shadrach, Meshach, and Abednego applied to Bobby's situation at his school. Then we talked about ways the song could apply to peer pressure situations in her life. After she understood the message, that song became her favorite.

Not long after we returned from that trip, Ann came home from school on a rainy day which had been spent almost entirely indoors. To pass the time during the lunch hour, the teacher had her pupils ask different questions. One little girl had asked, "How many watch MTV?"

Ann reported, "Everybody raised their hand but me."

I asked, "Why didn't you raise your hand?"

She said, "Because I don't watch MTV."

"Ann," I said, "that's nice. I'm very proud of you."

"But, Daddy," she said, Mary raised *her* hand, and she doesn't watch MTV either."

"Honey," I said, "why do you suppose Mary raised her hand?"

"Because she was probably afraid everybody would laugh at her."

I said, "You're probably right. So why didn't you raise *your* hand?"

"Because I don't watch MTV!" (My daughter is like her daddy. She is honest to a fault.)

Then I happened to remember our previous conversation about "Not Gonna Bow." I asked her, "Do you remember that song by Russ Taff?"

"Yeah," she answered.

"Do you remember how Bobby's friends wanted him to be just like them, getting him to compromise his standards? See how that relates to how you behaved in school today? Everyone was saying, 'Come on, Ann, won't you be like us!' And you said, 'I'm not gonna bow. I'm not going to bow to that pressure.' "

When I explained the significance of what she had done, she beamed with happiness. And I was excited about teaching spiritual values to my daughter through the medium of music.

At that point I began to let her listen to as much Christian music as I could. After she listens to a new tape, I ask her questions about the issues raised in the songs. I want her to think about the spiritual significance of everything she does, and these lessons come easiest through Christian music.

I take Christian music whenever we travel. Why listen to secular music when there is so much great Christian music to listen to? If I'm driving with one of my daughters, I always try to take along at least one tape with the spiritual values I'd like to communicate at that time. I also take one of her favorites, just in case she doesn't want to listen to mine. I might put on the first tape under the pretext that it's merely entertainment. But when it comes to a significant lyric, I ask, "Did you hear that?" I wait for her to respond yes or no. If she says no, I rewind it so she can hear it again. Then I ask her what it means.

To be honest, sometimes this approach works and sometimes it doesn't. If she isn't interested in a long discussion, I put her favorite tape in. But my daughters and I have had some of the deepest spiritual discussions about honesty, love, spiritual values, and the Christian life—all because music introduced the subject and we were able to discuss it right then and there.

One time we were listening to a song by Margaret Becker titled "Streets of Innocence" from her album *The Reckoning*. In the song, Margaret speaks of the joy of being morally innocent and reveals that her friends are often unable to sleep at night because they have compromised their values and principles. She sings, "You can have your money, you can have your fame, but I've got innocence and I can sleep at night."

When the song was through, my younger daughter Allison asked, "Daddy, what does 'innocence' mean?"

What a joy it was to share with her. I said, "Honey, you're innocent because you don't know how much pain sin can bring into your life. I can't really explain to you what it's like not to be innocent. But it's my prayer that you will remain innocent of sin and greed your whole life." Because of that song I was able to talk to her (for quite some time) about how God has made us innocent and how sin can wipe away that precious innocence.

Under normal circumstances, if I were to tell my daughter I wanted to talk to her about innocence, she would have a hard time sitting still. But because it was a topic she brought up, she sat in rapt attention as we discussed what was on her mind.

At another time, when Ann was eleven, she and I were listening to Kim Boyce's *Time and Again* album. This album contains a song called "Not for Me." I asked, "Do you understand what Kim is saying?"

She said yes and proceeded to explain it in detail. In the song Kim describes being tempted to go out with a non-Christian guy, but she decided against it because it could weaken her testimony and ruin her moral commitment. Even though she liked the guy, she decided not to see him.

After Ann thought for a while she asked, "Daddy, what's so wrong about going out with non-Christian guys? I don't plan on marrying one. But if I just want to go out on a date, non-Christian guys can be fun, too."

Here was an 11-year-old girl with a valid question, even though she won't be dating for five years. (We've already discussed the dating issue. I wanted her to wait until she was 37, but we compromised on 16.) I certainly took advantage of this opportunity for a long discussion of such an important matter. It was made much easier through the message of a Christian song.

Every once in a while, we hear of other families who are able to discuss important spiritual issues prompted by Christian music. For example, a father phoned my office one day asking for advice. He had a son who was slightly retarded and somewhat disabled, making it difficult for him to fit in with other boys his age. The father tried to help him feel comfortable with his friends as best he could.

The son had told his father that many of his friends listened to Bon Jovi, and the father was wondering if it was okay to purchase the music of that group for his son. We wouldn't recommend the sex-and-party mentality of this popular pop metal group, but we suggested that he might substitute a particular Christian group that had the same kind of sound, but also had a solid Christian message.

The father bought the tape we suggested and gave it to his son. The boy loved it. In fact, he took it with him to a weekend Boy Scout camp. When the other boys started to put Bon Jovi into their tape player, this young man said, "Hey, I have a better tape.

Let's listen to this. It's a Christian group and they're better than Bon Jovi."

"No way!" his buddies retorted.

"Yeah, it's true," said the boy. "Check this out."

They listened to it and they all really liked it. The Christian tape was a big hit all weekend.

As he was driving home from camp with his father, the young man went on and on about how neat the Christian rock band was and how the kids thought he was cool because of his tape. But the real turning point for the father was when his son turned and asked, "Dad, one of the songs on the tape talks about 'redemption.' What does that mean?"

For forty-five minutes, that father was able to explain the Gospel to his fourteen-year-old son and talk with him about his faith in Jesus Christ. He called us later, ecstatic, wondering if there were other groups he could encourage his son with.

SOME MUSIC DILEMMAS

Raising children is not all clichés and easy answers. More than once, I've had my theories about music put to the test. One time Ann asked if she could have a certain album by a relatively innocent secular performer. She had heard it at a girlfriend's house. I was not naive enough to think that she would never listen to secular music, but I was a little disappointed that she wanted to own this tape. She already had dozens of Christian tapes, including some that sounded very much like the secular artist she was asking for. What should I do? You would think if anyone had the answers, it would be me, right? Wrong. I was stumped, so I prayed for wisdom.

This was a situation where it would be a lot easier to think for the child than to challenge her to think for herself. As Ann's father, I had every right to tell her that I didn't want anything but Christian music in my house. But I didn't want to take the easy way out by making a decision without considering her.

We do have a rule in our home to avoid music which is against biblical values. But this artist didn't oppose biblical values. She was simply empty, not evil. So after much prayer and thought, I decided to challenge Ann to think through the situation and make her own decision. As we sat down to talk about it, I began to ask some questions: Why did she want this album when she knew I would not approve? Why did she want an album that looked at life from a perspective that left God out? Why did she want a non-Christian album when she already had so many good Christian albums?

As we talked, I realized I could never keep her from every influence of the world. I told her that my desire was to give her the strength to handle these situations on her own. The day will come when I no longer have control over her actions. If I don't teach her to think for herself now, how is she ever going to learn how to think when I'm not around?

I decided not to buy that album for her because I didn't believe it would be in her best interest. But I told her if she really wanted the album, she could buy it on her own. I also reminded her that I would buy any Christian album she wanted. I did find a new one that was very similar to the secular artist she liked. We listened to it together and discussed what she could learn from it.

Eventually, she decided she didn't want the secular album badly enough to spend her own money. In fact, her friend ended up buying the same Christian album I had purchased for Ann. My daughter had shared it with her and they both liked it better.

To be honest, I'm still not sure whether Ann changed her mind to please her daddy, because she really changed her attitude, or because she's cheap. All I know for sure is that she is still willing to discuss these things with me. I pray that will always be true.

By now my daughters have received dozens of Christian music tapes from their mom and me. They have enjoyed music from Kids Praise and G. T. and the Halo Express to Kim Boyce, Arcade, and Petra. But one day Ann wanted a Christian rock tape that I felt was too extreme for her tastes. I believed that some aspects of the group's appearance were unbecoming for Christians.

In the past when Ann had asked to listen to music or see movies and television programs that weren't appropriate for her, I explained why I refused and she had always understood. But this time after I explained my concerns about this group, she still wanted the tape. What should I do?

I didn't want to lose all communication with my independent-thinking daughter by insisting I was right. After all, I had always told her she could have any Christian tape she wanted. And this case wasn't a clear matter of right or wrong. It was a gray issue. But if I gave into Ann's wishes this time, would it be the beginning of more and more compromises? I thought being a parent was going to be easier than this!

I had already evaluated the tape by God's standards in Scripture and found no problem with the lyrics. They were spiritual and biblical. Nor could I argue that God wouldn't approve of the sound. I suspected that He might not approve of the group's appearance, but could I throw out the tape because I didn't approve of their appearance either?

I couldn't see anything wrong with this band for a young person already into this type of music. But my daughter was naive to this aggressive sound. I felt that a group like this might be too much for her. My biggest question was whether God would use this music in the life of my daughter.

It was at this point that my views on Christian music and Christian parenting came into conflict. The daddy in me still didn't want Ann to listen to this tape. I want my daughter to listen to Christian music that helps her focus on life from God's viewpoint. But as her parent, it's my responsibility to set guidelines for her. I challenged myself to pray and think this through.

I finally decided to give her the tape without the cover. I did this so she would have the music she wanted without being exposed to the group's appearance. It was a subtle reminder that I had reservations about the album. I also challenged her to evaluate her decision. Did she really want this album for ministry, enjoyment, or because I didn't want her to have it? She listened to the tape once or twice and put it aside. She hasn't listened to it since.

Now, for the record, this tape that caused me so much concern was the same one that had been so popular with the young Boy Scout and his friends at camp—the tape which had opened up a warm and fruitful conversation between that boy and his father concerning redemption in Jesus Christ our Lord.

I was certainly reminded that different musical styles reflect God's Word in different ways. What is suitable for one Christian's tastes may not be appropriate for another. And though I am responsible for my daughter's spiritual growth, I must be careful not to suppose that I always know what will minister to her.

I'm just glad there's so much good Christian music available to strengthen our spiritual walks. I'd like to challenge every Christian to use Christian music to revitalize his or her faith and joy in Jesus Christ.

THE INFLUENCE OF MUSIC

Sometimes we don't even realize to what extent music can influence us. I recall listening to one young man who poured out his fears and frustrations to me. He told me, "Every time I try to pray or read my Bible, wicked, sexual thoughts spring into my mind. I can't get rid of them, no matter how hard I try. It's frustrating. A Christian shouldn't have these thoughts. If I'm a Christian, I should be more like Christ."

Pat was a new Christian, one of several young Marines who attended the Sunday school class I taught. He had asked to talk with me in private, where he began to describe his troubles. Before he had become a Christian, these thoughts hadn't particularly bothered him. But now they had him completely discouraged.

"What kind of music do you listen to?" I asked.

"Why?" Pat asked, a puzzled look on

his face. "My music is not the problem. It's my thought life."

"Actually, you're struggling with your faith in Jesus and the joy of your salvation," I told him.

We read Colossians 2:8 together: "Don't let others spoil your faith and joy with their philosophies, their wrong and shallow answers built on men's thoughts and ideas, instead of on what Christ has said." (TLB).

Then I suggested, "Since most rock music is based on thoughts and ideas that oppose what Jesus taught, we need to look at the philosophies of the music you listen to." As we discussed Pat's listening habits, it became quite clear that they were having a negative effect on his thought life. His thoughts, in turn, were stifling his faith and joy about being a Christian.

I suggested that Pat put aside his sexual secular music for a while and substitute Christian music to see if the change would have any effect on his thought life. Sure enough, within a few weeks of changing his listening habits, Pat's entire demeanor changed. Over a period of time, we could see a positive attitude toward spiritual things develop in his life. His faith was growing. He began to view life from God's perspective instead of man's. The joy of his salvation returned. God was in the process of healing Pat's mind. Bible study, prayer, and Christian fellowship also became important elements of his renewal process.

"Why should I listen to music that will drag me down," Pat reasoned, "when I can listen to music that will heal instead?" Exactly! Today Pat is a seminary graduate and pastor of a growing church in the Chicago area.

A CHALLENGE TO OUR FAITH

It was becoming more and more obvious to me that many Christians needed a radical change in their musical habits if they were going to grow in Christ. At best, the secular music so many Christians listen to is "Twinkie music"—empty calories with no nutritional value. At worst, it can be absolute poison to their souls. That's why so many people have such a difficult time spiritually, emotionally, mentally, and morally. The music they feed on doesn't give them the strength they need to resist temptation, restore their faith and joy, and build strong spiritual muscles to experience victory in Christ.

Pat was one of the first people I ever

challenged to change his musical diet. Eventually the challenge evolved into what I call the 30-Day Christian Music Diet. It is a simple plan to change a person's thought life and deepen faith and joy in Jesus Christ by focusing exclusively on Christian music and media for a specific period of time.

We encourage all Christians to put away their secular entertainment and focus entirely on Christian music for 30 days. They should put away their secular records, CDs, cassettes, and videos. They should also switch off the TV, except for occasional newscasts they know won't conflict with biblical values.

How about you? Are you ready to take this challenge? If so, the easiest way to execute the plan is to get some Christian music cassettes to play in your car's tape deck or at home. If you can't find enough Christian music, then listen to teaching tapes from Christian speakers, read the Bible or Christian books, talk to your friends, talk to the Lord, or minister to the people around you. Plan your leisure hours to accomplish Christian purposes.

Completely surrender all your entertainment to the Lord. Fill your mind with the thoughts of Christ through Christian music. At the end of 30 days evaluate your spiritual life. How do you feel? How's your faith and joy in Christ? How's your thought life? Do you notice any significant changes in your attitudes and/or behaviors? Do your friends see a difference in you? After your evaluation, you can return to what you used to listen to. But it is my contention that you will experience a noticeable change. Many people who start on this strict Christian music diet never go back to their old forms of entertainment.

If it doesn't do anything else, the 30-day Christian Music Diet will create a gauge to help you measure your slavery to the world and your faith in Christ. I gave this challenge at a Christian youth convention, and many of the attendees decided to accept the challenge. But one young man came up to me in a panic. He acted like someone going through drug withdrawal, wringing his hands and complaining nervously. He told me, "It's been hard enough going without my music for the past two days. I know I can't make it for 30 days!"

What was he revealing about his faith? Although he wanted to get right with God, he was beginning to see that he was a slave to his music. Someone has said that if you have something you can't give away, you don't own it. It owns you.

Your ability to stick to the Christian Music Diet is an immediate measure of your attachment to the world. If the disci-pline to stay away from secular music does not come easily, it's a clue as to how much the music has a hold of your life. Everyone says they can take or leave something—until they actually have to leave it! It's like the guy who claims he can quit smoking any time. To prove it, he quit ten times just last week!

Entertainment can become a gauge that determines whether we are in the world or *of* the world. Are we moving through life directed by Christ, or does the world have its grip on us? We can't assume that just because we received Christ years ago that we will never fall under the influence of the world again. Whether teenagers, parents, or grandparents, we need to examine our lives regularly to see if the world has gained a hold on any part of our lives. Many Christians don't realize how dependent they are on the things of the world until they try to remove those influences from their lives.

The Christian Music Diet will also provide you with a yardstick to measure your faith in Christ. Too many people approach Christianity living as close to the edge as possible. It is a contest to see how much they can get away with. How far can they go before it's really sin?

We tend to believe that if there is nothing wrong with doing a certain thing, it must be right. But we should be asking, "How close can I come to Jesus Christ?" Anything that gets in the way must be set aside. Then our attitude becomes, "How far can I go to honor my Lord Jesus Christ?" We are no longer concerned with what's the least offensive thing a Christian can do, but what's the most holy thing a Christian can strive for.

Let's look at Paul's example. In Philippians 3, he makes a long list of his accomplishments, but immediately deems them all worthless compared to Christ and the power of His resurrection. He states over and over that he has not yet reached the place that he wants to be. And then he hits us with the zinger: "All of us who are mature should take such a view of things" (Philippians 3:15, NIV).

Here is Paul, one of the spiritual giants in the Bible, saying that a sign of maturity is admitting that you are in a continual process of growth. Your church may be a good one, and you may not be experiencing many problems in your personal life, but are these signs that your Christian life is all it could be? It's easy to mistake comfort for faith, or lack of trouble for God's blessing. Paul admonishes us to measure our faith by the fire of our commitment, not by how comfortable we are.

The best reason to participate in a 30-day Christian Music Diet is because it conforms to biblical guidelines. Paul tells us to take every thought captive for Jesus Christ (II Corinthians 10:5), which means we should consciously make an effort to monitor what goes into our brains. If we prayerfully evaluate our entertainment to see how much honors the Lord, we would find that many of the things we watch and listen to don't qualify.

DIETS DON'T WORK?

The average person today knows a lot about diets and the desire to lose weight. Who can avoid hearing about the Cambridge Diet, the Slim-Fast Diet, the Hollywood Diet, the Scarsdale Diet, the Weight Watcher's Diet, the Jenny Craig diet, and all the others? I frequently run into someone who claims to have tried them all, complaining that they just don't work. But that's not really true. Diets *do* work. Somewhere along the line, the failure to accomplish the desired goal rests on the person, not the diet.

A lot of people have the same skepticism about the 30-day Christian Music Diet. They ask, "Can't I listen to a little bit of secular music as long as I listen to mostly Christian music?" (In other words, "How much can I get away with?") I always respond with a question of my own: How many cookies does it take to ruin a diet? Then I illustrate the question with a personal story.

My mother-in-law, who is a wonderful cook, inevitably goes on a cooking binge just when I start a diet. Last time this happened, she was trying a new recipe for chocolate chip cookies—giant, soft, munchy, dripping, ready-to-melt-in-your-mouth chocolate chip cookies with an aroma that could make a strong man cry.

After I had completed a few successful days of my diet, Mom offered me one of her incredible edibles just out of the oven. "Al," she said, "I've just been doing a little baking. This is a new recipe. Try one."

I put up my hands. "Oh, I can't," I objected. "I just started a diet and chocolate chip cookies are definitely not on it."

"But I just baked them fresh for you and the girls," she said. "They're really good. Surely *one* won't spoil your diet."

I looked meekly at the plate of goodies and then at the face of my mother-in-law. She would be hurt and insulted if I didn't try one. And she was right—one cookie couldn't destroy my diet. "I'll just have one," I said bravely as I reached out for the sugary delight.

I had hardly enough time to enjoy the cookie before guilt set in. I realized with a pang of regret that I had just failed in my good intentions and had added fat to my body. In a panic, I ran to the scale in the bathroom and peered at the dial to determine how many pounds I had put on. It was amazing! The dial showed that I had gained no weight at all!

I felt better at once. I returned to the kitchen and was met by my mother-in-law with a plate in her hand. "Al," she says, "there are just two cookies left. Why not finish them off?"

Since I hadn't gained any weight from one cookie, I said, "Well, I guess I could." I snapped up both cookies and gobbled them down. Feeling guilty again, I ran back to the scales. Whew! I still hadn't gained any weight. Maybe I *would* be able to balance my diet with some of the things I like to eat.

But by then the floodgates had been opened. Soon I was not only eating cookies, but sampling my mother-in-law's German chocolate cake as well. Then I had some of her cherry pie. Before long I was eating pizza, Twinkies and everything else in the kitchen. *Snort, snort, grunt, grunt!* I had become a pig back at the trough and my diet was ruined.

I'm exaggerating just a little bit, but you get the point. How many cookies does it take to ruin a diet? Just one. The first one. It's not that one cookie alone destroys a diet, but it opens the door to accept all kinds of things that will. Only a strict diet works.

The same thing is true of a Christian music diet. Can't we just listen to a couple of secular albums or songs? No, because it only takes one musical Twinkie to counteract all the good that we are doing. Does the diet have to last an entire month? Yes, because it will take at least that long to establish the habit and start being healthy again.

Some people believe they can just stop

listening to the "bad" music. Rather than trying a complete Christian music diet, they suggest they can turn off the radio or skip any songs on their tapes and albums that are "bad." But this doesn't work for at least three reasons:

1) *Such a system is impractical.* Our music is usually just background accompaniment to other activities. We can't be turning the radio on and off, guessing how long the songs and commercials are. We're not going to keep interrupting other activities to skip a track on a record or CD, or to fast forward a tape. This system actually requires more discipline than it does to follow the diet.

2) *We may not be able to determine what constitutes a "bad" song.* We may have conformed so much to the world's value system that we are now entertaining ourselves with material that used to offend us. We no longer understand what is good in God's sight. If our faith and joy are suffering and we are spiritually out of shape, how perceptive can we be about what offends a most holy God?

3) *The "bad" songs aren't the problem.* If we had the spiritual discernment and discipline to stay away from the things that are spoiling our spiritual health, we'd already

be doing it! Telling someone who is struggling with faith and joy to turn off their bad music is like telling someone who is overweight to stop eating fattening foods. It doesn't work.

Dieters need to know what foods are fattening and what foods are right for them. Then they need a plan to get to their desired weight. They need a strict plan to follow. As long as they follow the plan, they need to put very little thought into the process. There is no longer any debate as to what they can get away with. I am suggesting the same kind of strict plan with the Christian Music Diet. Every compromise and excuse is a potential source of failure.

It's important to understand that no one at Al Menconi Ministries ever says that it's impossible to listen to secular music and still be a devoted Christian. We're not advocating hiding in the Christian media so the world will go away and not bother you anymore. We're not encouraging Christians to stick their heads in the sand and pretend the world doesn't exist. We know the world is out there. Christians are called to be in the world but not of it. However, many think they are not worldly, when actually the world has a strong grip on their lives. We hope to help strengthen their faith and joy so they can effectively minister in the world without being overtaken by its philosophies.

Nor have we ever said that eliminating secular music from your life will automatically make you spiritual. What we are saying is that you probably don't understand how much control the entertainment media has over you. And you will never fully understand until you completely step away from it. Of course, some people can listen to Christian music until they are blue in the face and it won't make any difference. The 30-day diet will only work for an individual who wants to serve Jesus and who wants to do what's best for a strong spiritual life.

SOME CASE HISTORIES

Tracy was probably the most rebellious girl in our Christian high school. She claimed to be a Christian, but once she told me in a counseling session, "Sometimes I even hate the name 'Christian.' It has been pushed down my throat since I was four."

Tracy was asked to leave school after her sophomore year because of her involvement with drugs. I didn't know or understand the full extent of Tracy's problems, but she wanted nothing to do with authority, Christianity, or further education. After leaving behind all church involvement and frequently running away from home, she finally awoke to her emptiness. She mistakenly thought she was pregnant and then saw how quickly her boyfriend wanted nothing to do with her. Tracy came face-to-face with the reality of a life without Jesus. At the age of 16, she could think of nothing worth living for.

But instead of committing suicide, she committed her life to Jesus. She became a new and different person inside. She petitioned the Christian school to let her return and complete her senior year. On campus, Tracy became a dynamo for Jesus. And thanks to her, I have at least one positive story to relate from a record burning.

In my counseling sessions with her, I didn't identify music as a major negative influence in her life, but she did. Tracy was one student who burned her rock records and didn't replace them. She testified in chapel that her old music had been a continual reinforcement of a rebellious lifestyle. In fact, burning her albums had allowed her to at last find the peace she had been seeking all her life. On her own, she had started a Christian music diet that helped her refocus her life on Christ.

Not long ago I was in the San Francisco area where a young man in his mid-twenties approached me. He said, "You don't know me, but I was a student at Moody Bible Institute when you spoke there a few years ago. I took your challenge to go on a 30-day Christian Music Diet because my faith and my joy weren't everything I wanted them to be. I knew something was wrong; I was just 'hanging on' spiritually. During the 30 days, if I couldn't find Christian music or entertainment, I turned everything off and sat quietly. I used that time to pray and meditate on the things of God, and I developed a new love for Jesus Christ. When I graduated from college, I became a church youth pastor. I was just going through the motions before, but now I have a deep love for my Lord."

The young man motioned toward a group of high school students. "Do you see all these young people?" he asked. "They are members of my youth group and I want to introduce them to you. They have also taken on the challenge to go on a 30-day Christian Music Diet! I can already see spiritual growth in many of them. It's all because you came to my college years ago and challenged us to go on a regular diet for the spiritual nourishment of our souls!"

THE CHALLENGE

Victory is possible in our lives and ministries, but not all of us are experiencing it. How about you? Perhaps you are one of many who will read this booklet, protesting at various points along the way: "Oh, that isn't for me," or, "But you don't under-stand," or, "Really, I don't listen to the words," or, "The music doesn't have a hold on my life," or, "I'm a nice person." Most of us tell ourselves all kinds of deceptive messages.

But right now, I would challenge you to honestly evaluate your faith and joy in Jesus Christ. Think back to your first encounter with Him, to the excitement and fervor you had when you became a Christian. You saw the world with such different eyes! Your mind and heart yearned for the things of God. Since those days, perhaps you have settled into a more apathetic, placid, inactive Christianity. Maybe you are going through the motions because they are now a habit, rather than being motivated by the Spirit's fire.

I challenge you to try the 30-day

Christian Music Diet—not because I think it is a magic formula nor because I think I have the right to climb into your soul to tell you what ministers to you. Rather, I challenge you to renew your first love. I want your faith and joy to be all it can be, and for you to have the passion for Christ you once had. I challenge you to move forward for Christ and become one of His warriors— not just a hearer of God's Word, but a doer also. And after you have done this and discovered what a difference it can make in your life, I pray that you will grow closer to your children by seeing that music is, indeed, a window to their souls.

Helping Families Grow Series

❦ *Communicating Spiritual Values Through Christian Music*

❦ *Equipping Your Child for Spiritual Warfare*

❦ *Family Vacations that Work*

❦ *Helping Your Child Stand Up to Peer Pressure*

❦ *How to Discover Your Child's Unique Gifts*

❦ *How to Work With Your Child's Teachers*

❦ *Helping Your Child Love to Read*

❦ *Improving Your Child's Self-Image*

❦ *Preparing for Your New Baby*

❦ *Should My Child Listen to Rock Music?*

❦ *Spiritual Growth Begins At Home*

❦ *Surviving the Terrible Teenage Years*

About the Author

Al Menconi is president of Al Menconi Ministries in Cardiff by the Sea, a small beach community near San Diego, California. He has been an acknowledged authority on the issues of music and ministry for over fifteen years, beginning when he was a Christian counselor and teacher. Al Menconi Ministries was founded in 1982 and now includes Media Update magazine, New Song Publishing, New Song Seminars, and other related resources for church, school, and home.

For more information, write:
Al Menconi Ministries
1635 S. Rancho Santa Fe Rd. #105
P.O. Box 5008
San Marcos, CA 92069
or call 619-591-4696.